BALTIC HOMES

INSPIRATIONAL INTERIORS FROM NORTHERN EUROPE

Sølvi dos Santos
Laura Gutman-Hanhivaara

With 262 colour illustrations

Thames & Hudson

Norwegian Sea

FINLAND

Gulf of Bothnia

SWEDEN

NORWAY

Oslo

Turku

Ekskär
187   207
         199   Helsink

Uppsala

31   47

Stockholm   Haapsalu

                                          173
                                                      P
                              Fårö   Saaremaa   161
                         53   39
                              63

                         Gotland   151
                                          Kipsala
                                                   Riga

DENMARK   Baltic Sea

              Copenhagen
                        73
North Sea   Ystad   Juodkrante 141   LITHUANIA
                   83   Curonian Spit

                        Bornholm   Vilni
                   95

              123
         Hiddensee   Rügen
                                        Sopot 131
    107   Gdańsk
Travemünde
         113
Lübeck   Germany   POLAND

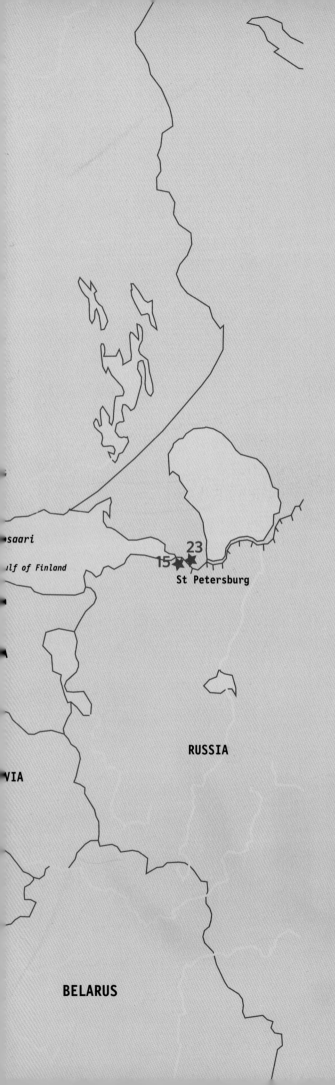

saari

lf of Finland

23

15

St Petersburg

RUSSIA

VIA

BELARUS

Contents

Baltic Vistas

Some winters you could practically cross it on foot. When the Baltic Sea freezes over it becomes a vast white sheet, utterly silent, penetrated only by the massive bulk of ice-breakers.

This unusual sweetness, due to the large rivers that drain their contents into the Baltic basin, means that the fishing is particularly good, with an abundance of sea and freshwater varieties alike. The coastal regions, like the islands and archipelagos, were inhabited until the 19th century by a scattering of fishermen and peasants. On the heathlands by the sea, sheep and horses have since time immemorial grazed the sparsely growing grass – a sharp contrast to the undulating plantations of rye, corn and flax that extend across the vast plain linking Germany, Poland and the Baltic lands. The farmhouses and fishermen's cottages were quite primitive constructions built of wood from the surrounding forests, and even the manor houses presiding over the various estates afforded no more than a modest degree of comfort. The towns of the Hanseatic League, built on river estuaries, sought to protect themselves against raids from the sea by erecting vast fortifications, above which the belltowers and gables of their town halls loomed up like landmarks for ships out at sea.

The history of the Baltic countries is that of a series of migrations and maritime conquests. The earliest explorers were the Vikings or Varangians who set out from present-day Sweden, Norway and Denmark, sometime before AD 800, and ventured as far as the coasts of Finland and Courland. Dealing in amber, skins and furs, they established a trading post at Visby on the island of Gotland. From the site of St Petersburg they travelled up the Neva to found the town and later principality of Novgorod, which was the origin of modern Russia (from Rus, or land of the 'red men' from Scandinavia).

In the 12th and 13th centuries, after they were converted to Christianity, the Danes pursued their colonial ambitions along the sea coast under the pretext of conducting a crusade against the pagans. By this means they captured Scania and the island of Rügen, established bases in Pomerania and later extended their possessions in Estonia. The magnificent 'age of the Valdemars' (1157–1241) saw the founding of both Copenhagen and Tallinn ('town of the Danes'). The founding of Lübeck in 1158–59 by Henry of Saxony provided a base for German merchants to expand their activities into the Baltic basin, where they established a series of outposts for their various companies. These were overseen by associates, often family members, who represented their interests in the new trading 'counters'. Riga and Königsberg (Kaliningrad), founded in 1201 and 1255 respectively, and Danzig (Gdańsk) and Reval (Tallinn), acquired in 1309 and 1346, were among the fortified towns under the control of German overlords who formed part of the Hanseatic League.

The last obstacle to the Christianization of the region was the pagan Grand Duchy of Lithuania, which extended as far as the Black Sea. In 1395, with the aim of denying the Teutonic Knights the pretext of mounting a crusade against them, the country adopted the Catholic religion and formed a union with the kingdom of Poland. With the decline of the League, in the 16th century the battle for control of the region was waged anew, this time between Denmark and Sweden, which had both become Protestant, Poland, which had remained Catholic, and Orthodox Russia. In the 17th century, under the Vasas, Sweden became the dominant force in the Baltic, which was almost transformed into a 'Swedish lake'.

In the 18th century, the Swedish spoils were divided between the German states and the Russia of Peter the Great, who founded St Petersburg and annexed the Baltic provinces. A century later, Napoleon and Tsar Alexander III joined forces to launch an attack on the last of the Swedish possessions, and Russia seized Finland. Under the Tsar's authority, Estonians, Livonians (Latvians), Lithuanians and Finns experienced broadly the same fate as the Russians themselves, while Poland, split between Germany, Austria and Russia, disappeared off the map altogether.

As a consequence of World War I and the Bolshevik Revolution, Russia was forced to withdraw from the region, and the 1920s saw the emergence of the new nations of Lithuania, Latvia, Estonia and Finland. The Nazi–Soviet Pact of 1939 brought this brief interval of freedom to a tragic end. Annexed by the USSR, they were occupied by Germany and came once again under Soviet domination. Their independence was restored in the so-called 'singing revolution' of 1991, which paved the way for entry to the European Union in 2004.

The Baltic lands are the common heirs to a tumultuous history, as we can tell from a piece of Gustavian furniture or a brine cask, say, that turns up far from its place of origin. The constant to and fro of maritime trade has helped to forge a regional identity enriched by a shared patrimony.

Today, people readily appreciate the sheer beauty of the long sandy beaches at the forest's edge and the innumerable granite islands of the archipelagos. Romantic late 19th-century villas are being restored, with their turrets, balconies and verandas, and as often as not a landing stage and matching wooden pavilion in the garden. But whether farmhouses, sailors' cottages, manor houses nestled in their vast estates or modern dwellings perfectly integrated with the natural environment, the houses of the Baltic proclaim their heritage out loud. From Denmark to Sweden, Poland, Russia, Finland or Estonia, from Germany to Lithuania or Latvia, local idiosyncrasies and common traditions are spelled out in an intricate symbiosis. In these northern lands, where the cold and the darkness are succeeded by brilliant sunshine, Midsummer's Day is the traditional occasion to celebrate the return of the fine weather – and there is much to celebrate in this unpretentious and sociable lifestyle of sailing and yacht races, fantastic fishing and long-drawn-out dinners with friends.

Sweden

The most famous of the races organized by the fashionable Royal Swedish Yacht Club (KSSS) is the Gotland Runt, which takes place every year at the beginning of summer. Three hundred yachts set sail from Sandhamn on the Stockholm archipelago on a course that takes them right round the island of Gotland. The event attracts a huge following, with many spectators putting to sea in their own craft or watching from the port of Visby. The Swedish passion for sailing comes as no surprise, of course, given that mastery of the seas has been the key to their history ever since the Vikings.

Modern Sweden has managed to hang on to a number of its disputed offshore territories, among them the islands of Öland, Gotland and its tiny neighbour Fårö, which are much prized today as holiday locations. Gotland's handsome stone houses are reminders of the island's trading past, the multicoloured façades and walls of the buildings reflecting its former pros-perity. In the altogether gentler climate of Sweden's southernmost region, the habitat was radically different, and the great plains of Scania were soon studded with farmsteads – not unlike the one from which naughty young Nils Holgers-son is supposed to have made his escape on the back of his white gander!

These farmhouses are much in demand by today's city-dwellers who want a bolt hole in the country but love the proximity to Malmö and Copenhagen, now within easy reach since a bridge was built linking southern Sweden with Denmark. Even in Stockholm, situated as it is on an archipelago, it is possible to live by the sea and sail out to one of the islands for a few days. It could be in a 19th-century villa or an ecologically sound modern masterpiece. What people are looking for is the chance to recharge their batteries, to get back to nature and a simpler life where there is time for sunshine, hospitality and friendship.

PAGES 26–27: A view of the Stockholm archipelago.

OPPOSITE: Highly characteristic of Fårö are the ghostly shapes of limestone rocks, eaten away by the ice that envelops them in the long winter months.
RIGHT: The window of a traditional Gotland house.

A remarkable collection
of old farmhouse
furniture gives
the seaside home
of a Swedish shipowner
its rustic feel.

For this Swedish shipowner, a maritime setting was pretty much a foregone conclusion. When he acquired a holiday home on the Stockholm archipelago, of course it was the sea view he was looking for. But relaxing on the veranda for a few hours watching the yachts go by was not what he had in mind: he wanted to be able to see that view from every room in the house! Walls were knocked down, and four partitioned rooms merged into a single space that opened, at ground-floor level, on to the covered veranda, from where there is an extraordinary view of the archipelago. The only thing spared was the staircase, which was left intact in its original colours.

The house has been modernized and insulated, and a proper heating system installed, making it possible to live there all year round, but it has not been furnished in a contemporary style. The owner is a great lover of Swedish antique furniture and has built up an astonishing collection over the last twenty years, scouring sale-rooms, auctions and antique shops. This acquisitive streak goes back to childhood. The lamp that hangs above the stairs, which he brought back as a small boy from a voyage to Brazil on his grandfather's yacht, bears testament to this.

The old farmhouse furniture and primitive paintings from Dalecarlia that give this house its rustic feel are now almost impossible to find. The superb Swedish wall-hangings – because they used to be taken out of the chests where they were stored all year and hung on the walls only for special occasions – have retained all the freshness of their original colours. They are their new owner's pride and joy.

Everywhere, the maritime theme crops up again: hanging in the veranda is the model of a ship, of the type once used as a votive offering in the churches of seaside villages to keep their menfolk safe from harm. There is also a copper porthole converted into a mirror and, on every wall, amateur paintings of ships by sailors, immensely touching in their painstaking concern to render every last detail. You hazard a guess that our shipowner, marooned on dry land, wants a constant reminder of the freedom he associates with life at sea.

PAGE 30: One of the small guest houses, seen from the small terrace outside the front door.

ABOVE AND OPPOSITE: At one time, the lives of the inhabitants of these coastal regions revolved around sailing and boatbuilding. Models of ships, similar to the one on the veranda (opposite) and sometimes of threatening proportions, were hung from church roofs; prayers inscribed on the hull asked for divine protection against bad weather, the perils of war or piracy. These models are now collector's items, much sought after by sailing enthusiasts, shipowners, yachtsmen and amateur sailors. The paintings of sailing ships (above) were done by sailors to pass the time on long voyages.

PAGES 38–39: Inspired by the local wooden farmhouses, Helen and Marcus's house differs only in respect of its large windows, which are designed to let in as much light as possible.

OPPOSITE: When the wind whistles or the winter is too severe, everyone huddles round the hearth. On the mantelshelf are displayed pieces of ceramic, pebbles and driftwood from the beach (detail above), all of local origin!

RIGHT: Sheepskin – which keeps Swedish babies snug in their straw baskets – is used here to make seat covers for the dining chairs (bottom right), while a stool found in Dalecarlia (top right) is covered in cowhide.

ABOVE AND OPPOSITE: A beautiful light and airy open space – that was the ultimate goal to be kept in mind during the construction of the house, which was designed in close cooperation with an architect friend. Gone are the days of tiny kitchens relegated to the end of a corridor behind closed doors. The large open-plan kitchen (opposite) is simple and functional and ideal for socializing. The bathroom (above) required a bit more in the way of privacy and was therefore provided with a door.

OVERLEAF: The wild, rugged shoreline of Fårö.

This handsome white
early 20th-century villa
on the Stockholm archipelago
is redolent with period
charm, as haunting as the
scent of roses....

Three children in sailor suits occupy the white boat being steered by a young man through the waters of the Stockholm archipelago. The family photograph perfectly captures the elegance and carefree atmosphere of Sweden before the outbreak of World War I. In 1912, Erik Hirsch, who made his fortune by inventing the milk separator, had a villa built on the small island of Stegesund, designed by Ivar Tengbom. At the time, he had of course no idea that his young architect was to become a leading practitioner of the art in the 1920s, famous for his stripped-down classical style.

Hirsch's house is in fact representative of the prevailing Art Nouveau of which Tengbom, an avid devourer of the English periodical *The Studio*, was particularly enamoured at the time. Granted, the handsome fluted Doric columns flanking the main entrance and supporting the porch do anticipate the classical style the architect subsequently developed, but the sloping roofs and organic outlines of the house are the living proof of his perfect mastery of Art Nouveau. The spacious white interior, logically distributed around the staircase, corresponds to the principles of clarity and simplicity laid down by Viollet-le-Duc and John Ruskin. White furniture and Liberty wallpaper complete the look, with the addition of a few Biedermeier touches. It is all very much in the spirit of Sundborn, home of the painter Carl Larsson – which was familiar to the whole of Sweden via his delightful watercolours – but transformed by the subtlety of the detailing.

Nothing much has altered since the grandfather's day, except perhaps the steamboats that once served the islands. In the garden arbours, you almost think you catch sight of elegant women from the early 20th century sipping their tea out of Swedish china from Rörstrand.... For the moment the summer term ended, the Hirsch family would ensconce themselves in their summer quarters at Solgård (Sun House), taking along all the staff and condemning papa to commute to and fro from Stockholm. A farm supplied the kitchens with meat and eggs, while the greenhouse and the vegetable garden provided all the fruit and vegetables needed for island life. Today the grandson of Erik Hirsch, Per Wästberg, is a member of the Swedish Academy, and he has appointed himself the chronicler of this summer paradise as his grandfather experienced it during the thirties. He describes the passion with which they all took up sailing and participated in the excessively smart regattas organized by the Royal Swedish Yacht Club (KSSS). The family album contains photos of Erik Hirsch having coffee on his yacht, *Ta-Ta*, surrounded by members of the crew. Amusing also to imagine the gentlemen out on the porch smoking a cigar after dinner, while the ladies perched on cane chairs, enveloped in their shawls.

Time has not stood still at Solgård, where the sound of children's laughter is perhaps more common today than it was in the past. Yet the garden is still full of roses and the Rörstrand china is still brought out at teatime. New generations take up sailing, and the pages of the family album fill up with images of present happiness.

ABOVE AND RIGHT: One of Solgård's
most striking features is the sense
of unity that prevails throughout.
Because Ivar Tengbom, its architect,
was inspired by the Arts and Crafts
Movement, he viewed the house
as a totality: the sideboard in the
dining room (above) and mirrored
wardrobe in the bedroom (right) were
designed specifically to match the
style of architecture. Proportions,
materials for furniture, fabrics and
wallpaper are all in perfect harmony.
One survivor from the Gustavian
age is the Swedish stove (above)
which calls to mind the blue and
white china of the Rörstrand factory.

PAGES 46–47 AND OVERLEAF: Idyllic
views from the bedrooms over the
Stockholm archipelago.

Every house in Gotland contains some small treasure from the island's Viking past.

Anders Palmér is an artist, more specifically a landscape painter, who for some twenty years now has found his inspiration on the island of Gotland. As his paintings are often of very large proportions, he does not use an easel but paints on to a flat canvas unrolled directly on the stony ground. The titles of his works are like an invitation to his collectors to come to Gotland and see for themselves. It was a girlfriend who originally brought him to spend a holiday on the island, then unknown to him as he had always spent the summer at the family home in Skåne (Scania). He began to dream about having a house there where he could go to paint for half the year. In the event his wish was granted as the result of a complete coincidence, when a friend took him along to pick up the keys of a house he was renting on the island. It just so happened that the house next door was for sale, and Anders made up his mind then and there: although he had barely even seen it, this was the house for him.

Renovating the building, which for a long time had only been used for storage, took him ten years. In reinforcing the walls, traces of the original colours were revealed, including a façade of a reddish ochre that matched the setting sun. One of Anders's great pleasures is to pass the long summer evenings on the terrace that has been created inside the stone walls of what was once a kitchen.

The house is not large: just an entrance hall, a kitchen and two rooms. Our painter therefore decided to make himself a bedroom under the eaves, retaining the bare stone walls. The ground-floor rooms were repainted in the colours they had originally boasted three hundred years ago, a time when the use of such pigments was a mark of wealth. Wall alcoves once used for storing food are now the home for books and decorative objects. But Anders has really not changed very much else, as the last thing he wanted was to introduce into a 17th/18th-century house the sort of modernity he feels at home with in Stockholm. Instead he has managed to track down copies of the furniture at Gripsholm Castle, a style he regards as much more in keeping with the decor of the Gotland house.

History is all around you on this peaceful Baltic island. Up to the time of the Danish invasion, before the German traders brought prosperity to its capital of Visby, Gotland was the fiefdom of the Vikings. Chance archaeological finds are commonplace on the island and Anders's neighbours proudly display rusty old nails, keys and knives. He himself likes to speculate on the treasures that still lie hidden from prying eyes, for his house was built on the estate known as Hägvards, in the north-west of the island, and stands on the foundations of an old Viking farm. Echoes of this ancient and mythic past may be deciphered in the Gotland painter's works.

ABOVE: Gotland is the southernmost of the Swedish provinces and the one where the sun shines longest – hence perhaps the rather Provençal feel of the terrace. It is the site for many a delightful evening as the collapsed stonework of the former kitchen retains the heat of the day. Beyond it lies a garden which provides all the aromatic herbs needed for the kitchen. Anders believes his recent passion for Tuscany, where he currently teaches and paints for half the year, has its roots in these summers spent on the Swedish island.

OPPOSITE: In the bedroom built under the eaves, the stone walls have been left in their original condition.

PAGES 56–57: The sitting room.

OPPOSITE AND RIGHT: The blue sitting room (opposite) dates from the 17th century and is part of the original house, although the traces of a fresco on the wall above the fireplace are of more recent origin. To the left is an alcove, today used purely for display purposes but once a place to store jams at a constant temperature. The dining room (top right) occupies an 18th-century extension. If you add to this the entrance hall, red with a simple band of grey, and the kitchen in almond green (bottom right), all of Gotland's traditional colours are represented. The attractive odd set of blue and white crockery was sought out item by item in second-hand shops and salerooms.

ABOVE AND LEFT: The island of Gotland has as many sheep as it does human inhabitants! The dry, rocky soil of the Baltic islands makes agriculture difficult but the heathland provides the flocks with huge pastures, their boundaries marked by dry-stone walls made of the characteristic Gotland limestone (left).

OPPOSITE (TOP): Bunches of flax hung out to dry on a wooden frame, ready to be woven during the winter months.

OPPOSITE (BOTTOM): Nineteenth-century wooden houses and German-influenced half-timbered farmhouses make up the island's housing stock.

It is called Spring House, *Gaustäde* in Gotland's curious Swedish dialect, with its admixture of Danish, German and even Russian – a vivid illustration in itself of the way this island at the heart of the Baltic was fought over by the coastal powers in the age of the Vikings and under the Hanseatic League. Since 1645, the island has belonged to Sweden, and this limestone house with its tiled roof dates all the way back to that period of the 17th century when wood was kept solely for shipbuilding, and there would have been no question of putting up a wooden house or even of panelling its interior. The solid stone walls of Gaustäde were therefore painted in bright colours: blue picked out in red for the outside door and window apertures, and yellow, red and green in combination with grey-blue for the interiors. Ultramarine and cobalt blue were particularly favoured, especially for kitchens, where they were thought to deter flies. Over the last six years, all the rooms at Gaustäde have been restored to their original colours, thanks to work undertaken in part by the Commission for Historic Monuments and in part by Eva's father. Everything has been done by the book, using natural pigments mixed with oil and egg.

Not that this was the first house Eva's father had done up. A former funeral mason, it was something he had been used to doing all his life. When he was a young man, he met his future wife on Gotland, and the two of them determined to return there when they retired. Now it is on his daughter's behalf that he has been slaving away, first finding and then restoring the house, and tracking down furniture on the island.

For Eva Darpö, Gotland is a reminder of her grandmother and the source of inspiration for her work as an artist.

Eva used to spend her summers as a child on the neighbouring small island of Fårö in her grandmother's old windmill, which consisted of round rooms on a number of levels. What she wanted for herself was a space where she could still spend the holidays with her family but also have somewhere to work with glass and ceramics, and to exhibit. With its outbuildings, Gaustäde in the small village of Fårösund, in the north of the island, fulfilled all her requirements. The main house was used as the living space, while Eva installed her studio in what was once the forge and transformed the stables into a gallery, where she exhibits her sculptures every summer alongside paintings by various friends, among them Anders Palmér.

Although she would be hard pressed to say exactly how, the island of Gotland has a strong influence on her work. It may be the penetrating summer light, the arid heathland dominated by heavy skies, or the greyish tinge that clings to all the colours – Eva finds it impossible to say. The flash of the waves and the luminosity of the first white flowers of summer never cease to amaze her. Or, who knows, it may just conceivably be something in the water…. Could it be from the spring at Gaustäde that she draws her inspiration?

PAGES 64–65: The small dining room.

ABOVE AND RIGHT: On a rococo chair
are some of the glasses made by Eva
Darpö in her workshop. She also uses
the furnace to make her wonderfully
insubstantial sculptures of birds.
OPPOSITE: Great care went into the
restoration of the wall decorations
in the formal dining room (in the
foreground), which consist of a
painted frieze running along the top
of the wall and a broad band of grey at
the base, in the manner of a plinth.
The original flooring had been used
for firewood, so it was replaced with
antiqued wooden boards, often left
bare, as in the small dining room
(pages 64–65). In the other rooms,
as in most northern interiors, woven
rag runners protect the floors.

Opposite and Above: Eva is sensitive to the house's particular atmosphere and takes care that everything in the way of decorative objects and furniture is old, whether it belonged to her grandmother or was spotted on the island or brought in from one of the other Swedish provinces – as is the case with the wooden bench covered in sheepskin (opposite, in the kitchen). In the country that was where people used to sleep in preference to using a proper bed; some were even made with an extension that could be folded away during the day.

The 17th-century paving stones in the kitchen are virtually unscathed. In the back kitchen (above), a chest covered by a woollen tapestry is set in front of the open fire once used both for heating this part of the house and for cooking.

Overleaf: Boathouses on the Fårö shore.

PAGES 76–77: The bedroom features an original tiled stove.

ABOVE AND OPPOSITE: When Barbro scours the antique shops, she tries to distinguish between the pieces she wants to keep and things she will sell on. But it never pays to be too sentimental, and the famous rococo sofa that started off the whole crazy adventure was actually sold last spring and replaced with a large bench-style sofa with simple jute cushions (opposite).

As in most Nordic houses, the windows are curtainless. The internal shutters in the salon are original.

Elisabeth Holte opens the door of her house, lets the cats in and perches on the step to look out over the plain stretching before her to the horizon. Here she can draw a deep breath and forget the kilometres she has covered on the journey from Norway to this part of the Swedish countryside on the southernmost tip of Skåne. Elisabeth bought the house when she was the Stockholm correspondent for a Norwegian daily newspaper. She had long wanted a home of her own, and found exactly what she wanted with the help of a lawyer in Skåne. The Norwegians speak of this region in the same breath as Tuscany because of the sweetness of the landscape: fields of blue flax in spring and yellow rape in summer, sheep, and long sandy beaches on the Baltic that have no counterpart in Norway. Once night has come, when the plain is plunged into darkness and the lights of the farmhouses twinkle in the distance, like the lights of ships that are strangely becalmed, Elisabeth has the sensation of being out on the open sea. What could be more attractive than to light the candles of the gilded chandelier suspended from the branches of her magnificent oak tree and pass some time with her friends, nearby farmers and the artists and antique dealers who have come in their numbers to set up home in Skåne. This is a place where the peace of the country and a cultural life go hand in hand: one day out in the fields, the next at a private view in Simrishamn or Ystad.

The biggest compliment you can pay her is to assume, quite sincerely, that the house is older than it really is, so successfully has Elisabeth recreated the character of a local farmhouse. Little more than an empty shell, it had provided a modest home for two peasant families since it was built in 1917. Although it had to be renovated from top to bottom, not a sign of the work remains. The small whitewashed farmhouse with a slate roof was extended to take in the old barn that lay at right angles to the dwelling house. With the four original rooms plus three new ones, Elisabeth has space for the treasures brought back from her travels all over the world, many of these authentic peasant pieces picked up for a song. She has given the interior warmth and interest by using old mattress ticking with red stripes for cushion covers, while terracotta egg plates (used for chopped bacon omelettes with blueberry jam) serve as her everyday crockery. Digging around in antique and second-hand shops is one of her hobbies, and her eagle eye is capable of spotting amazing finds tucked away at the bottom of some old peasant chest.

Daydreaming, strolling over the vast beaches nearby, walking to the lighthouse at Sandhammaren, that is how she spends most of her time when she is far removed from the stresses and strains of the town and the full diary that goes with her job as editor of a Norwegian interior decoration magazine. Before she leaves, Elisabeth casts one last look round the small courtyard, which is paved with pebbles dug up out of the fields during the building work, and it seems to sum up everything that draws her back.

It was no more than an empty shell set in beautiful countryside when a Norwegian journalist set about turning it into a proper home that reflected her own taste and enthusiasms.

Denmark owes its wealth and influence to the strategic position it occupies between the Baltic and the North Sea. Although most of its territory lies on the Jutland peninsula, the establishment of the capital at Copenhagen, on one of the 406 islands, reflects the crucial importance of its straits – passage through which was made subject to a royal tax as far back as 1429. So vital was the narrow route off Elsinore that the proceeds from the so-called Sound Duty enabled Denmark to dominate mercantile traffic in the Baltic right up to the 18th century.

The Danish kings at first extended their conquests out to the west – where in the early part of the 11th century they founded an Anglo-Danish empire – and then at the end of the 12th century towards Estonia and Courland. In 1397, the Union of Kalmar brought all the Scandinavian kingdoms under their dominion. When the Danes lost Sweden in the 16th century, the inhabitants of the island of Bornholm refused to submit to their new masters; they took the Swedish Lieutenant-Governor prisoner and killed him when he tried to escape. A delegation went to Copenhagen to swear allegiance to the Danish King.

At the heart of the Baltic, Bornholm offers two contrasting types of landscape. The north, with its eroded rocky coastline, has a Scandinavian character, while the sandy shores in the south are typical of the beautiful beaches on the Baltic mainland. The most wooded of all Denmark's provinces, the island is also famous for its traditional herring smokehouses and windmills.

PAGES 90–91: Farms strung out over the undulating plain on Bornholm's eastern side.

OPPOSITE AND RIGHT: Wheat and oats are Bornholm's main crops, and the island has deposits of kaolin clay, used locally in the manufacture of ceramics.

Do you need to be born in the Baltic to live there on an island all year round? Or is it some mad desire for freedom that makes the isolation so appealing?

Finn is a sea captain, and when he goes to sea, Jette Iversen never forgets to turn the two little china dogs that stand in the window to face the road, so they can wait there faithfully for their master's return. In so doing she is carrying on the ritual inherited from her grandmother, also a captain's wife on Bornholm. For Jette, who had left Bornholm, returning to the island where she was born was for a long time a distant dream, but one she was finally able to realize in 1979 when she bought a house in Salmon Street in Rønne, the island's principal town. A few years later, Finn moved into the house across the road. When the pair decided to live together, they kept both houses so that family and friends could come and stay in the holidays.

Though built in 1830 and 1850 respectively, the two houses are identical, long and low, distinguished only by a half-timbered rear façade to the older building. In one of the gardens where Jette lovingly tends her flowers and vegetable plot, the mild climate has allowed her to grow a vine and even a magnificent fig tree.

When she moved back to the island of Bornholm, Jette bought nothing. She was content either to recycle or design the furniture she needed. In her parents' home, for example, she found an unfinished wooden bench her father had intended to give her mother before they were married. She put all the pieces back together and painted it black. The portraits of her grandparents hanging on the wall are the record of her family history, and also the symbol of her personal stake in the island. In Finn's house, Jette has preferred to use modern furniture, and she has chosen the best Denmark has to offer: Arne Jacobsen. No more than a minute away from each other, as far as everyday living is concerned the two houses function as one, with each retaining its own particular atmosphere and traditions.

'A Bornholmer,' explains Jette with a laugh, 'is an inhabitant of Bornholm, a pendulum clock and a smoked herring!' A Bornholmer all year round, Jette enjoys her houses and gardens, with their views of windmills and the tall white chimneys of the fish smokehouses. Even if she sometimes feels the need to leap on the boat and go to Copenhagen to breathe the air of the capital, on the island she has a very strong sense of her identity as an island-dweller. This is home, her own little bit of happiness.

PAGE 94: A view of the entrance hall in Finn's house.

ABOVE AND RIGHT: On Bornholm, the traditional method of construction is half-timbering according to the German model. Because of the many windows that punctuate their façades, the houses in Salmon Street (above) – the prettiest in town – benefit from natural light all day long. Ecological correctness dictates the use of bicycles (right).

OPPOSITE: Ceramics, textiles and glassblowing are among Bornholm's traditional crafts. Before becoming an architect, Jette learned the technique of glassblowing, although her interest is now confined to the collection of antique glass that occupies the windowsills, the ideal location to show off the iridescent transparency of decanters, goblets and flagons.

ABOVE AND RIGHT: The island of Bornholm is Denmark's most wooded province and Almindigen, at the heart of the island, is the country's second largest forest. When Jette's father retired, he became an enthusiastic wood-turner, producing plates, bowls, cups and eggs for his daughter.
OPPOSITE: In the kitchen, an ironmonger's cabinet discovered in Copenhagen has been converted into a work surface. Children are fascinated by its many drawers and delight in speculating about the items they once contained.

OPPOSITE AND ABOVE: It was sheer chance that brought about Dr Marwitz's association with German sculptor Alex Cassel, whose sister happened to be one of his patients. Knowing of her dentist's tastes as a collector, she showed him some of her brother's exhibition catalogues.

He was immediately so taken with what he saw that he went straight to see Cassel in Normandy, and bought his first piece – an elongated human figure that reminded him of totemic figures he had come across in the course of travels overseas (above). A friendship sprang up between the two men, punctuated by meetings and further acquisitions (opposite).

Dr Marwitz particularly enjoys the different views of his artworks afforded by the maze of stairways and corridors.

OPPOSITE: Twice a year, the collector holds a big party for up to fifty people, which is the opportunity for him to show off his latest passions. A sculpture by Cassel stands outside the dining room, in which it is possible to see a rocket-shaped sculpture by Irmer on the wall.

ABOVE: On the top floor, below the roof terrace, other sculptures by Alex Cassel have found their home in Dr Marwitz's vast bedroom. A sliding glass door leads to the en-suite bathroom.

RIGHT: The library contains a fine selection of art books, as well as a reclining chair by Le Corbusier.

Young Erik Krettek is just sixteen years old. He spends all his summers on the barge bought by his family eleven years ago in Potsdam. It is called *The Patriot*, a name that conjures up Germany's military past. Given its dilapidated state when they purchased it, architect Steffi Weihrauch and her husband Udo Krettek, a former engineer, had to call on all their skills to restore it to its original glory bit by bit and repair the few furnishings that remained.

To accommodate both Erik's family and his uncle's, five bedrooms were needed, as well as a bathroom, kitchen, DIY space and, most important, several reception rooms, allowing space for everyone to relax in their own way – although actually the best moments of all tend to be those spent out on the deck, just letting time pass by. Lacking a motor, the barge is permanently moored, but no matter – Erik can still get out his rod or skim stones without leaving home. But as it would be just too cruel to be at sea without going anywhere, a small motorboat is available for trips in the Baltic and for Erik to go fishing with his father.

Painted white, bright
blue and black, a barge
moored on the island
of Hiddensee is an
invitation to laze away
the days under the wide
open skies of Pomerania.

Getting *The Patriot* to Hiddensee was a major performance as it had to be towed along every river lying between Potsdam and the Baltic. Fortunately, making the trip to Rostock for the five-yearly refurbishment is not so difficult. Normally, when you come to Hiddensee by road from Berlin, you have to leave the car on the mainland and catch a ferry out to the island. In winter, though, when you come to check the barge is in good shape, you can drive right up to it over the frozen ice. And what a delight it is in summer to live on an island where there are no cars, so you go everywhere by bicycle, and you can watch the horses roaming free on the plain.

The nearby island of Rügen, immortalized by the German Romantic painter Caspar David Friedrich, is frankly not to Erik's taste, and he tends to drag his heels when his parents go there for the weekend. Yet it is a delightful place, with wooden villas, white chalk cliffs, beech forests and little villages with thatched farmhouses. In a previous age, the British writer and adventurer Elisabeth von Arnim, a Pomeranian by marriage, used to come here in search of peace and quiet. But these tales of the past do not mean a whole lot to this young man, who prefers his unsophisticated little island by a long chalk.

PAGES 120–121: The barge's mooring, behind the dunes.

PAGE 122: The kitchen opens on to the main sitting room, where everyone likes to gather round the fire when the evenings are cool.

ABOVE AND OPPOSITE: Suspended between sky and sea, the barge rocks almost imperceptibly at its mooring, so calm is the Baltic in summer. When carrying out the restoration work, Steffi Weihrauch sought out the old furniture and well-worn materials that give the interior its unpretentious appearance.

Accommodation was needed for the two families who share the barge, hence the large number of bedrooms. All are very simply furnished, with just a few reminders that this is a boat and not a house.

LEFT: On the island of Hiddensee, people are ecologically minded. There is no access for cars, and everyone either uses a bicycle or walks.

Poland

Although most people still have a clear mental image of the shipyards at Gdańsk, from the dramatic days of Lech Walesa and the Solidarity movement, they know very little else about Poland's busy maritime capital. But refer to Gdańsk by its former name of Danzig, and a whole other set of associations springs to mind – the Free City, the granary of Europe, the trading centre that was crucial to the expansionist activities of the German merchants of the Hanseatic League. Situated at the mouth of the Vistula, its port has always been Pomerania's outlet to the sea – a state of affairs that continued right up to the 20th century, when the new port of Gdynia was built less than twenty kilometres away.

In the 14th century, Pomerania was under the control of the Teutonic Knights, eventually defeated with the help of the Polish King in the 15th century. The massive fortress of Marien-burg, or Malbork, former headquarters of the Grand Masters of the Order, is the continuing proof of their power and influence in that era. Danzig, although its fate was intimately bound up with the Hanseatic League, nevertheless enjoyed independent status, right up to the time of its annexation by Prussia in 1772, on the occasion of the second partition of Poland. The town briefly regained its privileged position as an independent city under the protection of Napoleon, and then once again in the 1920s.

Günter Grass, born in Danzig in 1927, remembers an age when the town was still essentially German, before World War II changed the course of its history. One thing that has not changed is the landscape of the great Pomeranian plain with its undulating fields of rye. Near Gdańsk, the coastal region is particularly attractive with gently sloping mountains.

PAGES 126–127: Fishing boats at Sopot.

OPPOSITE: A view of Gdańsk, where the houses line the banks of the river Vistula and the many canals crisscrossing the town.
RIGHT: Architectural details and a Baroque door reflect the Germanic past of the former Danzig.

With its prestigious address on Heroes of Monte Cassino Street in Sopot, Eva and Michal's restaurant is the talk of the town.

Once upon a time, there was a doctor from Alsace serving in Napoleon's army called Jean Haffner, who believed that the waters of the Baltic Sea had healthgiving properties. This set him thinking about opening a spa on the outskirts of Danzig, and while the town was still under French protection, he acquired land in Sopot. Then, when the Empire fell and Prussian rule was restored, this same Dr Haffner built first his baths, in 1823, and in the following year a thermal spa, with beautiful parks and, above all, the big wooden pier which was to become the town's fashionable walking place and its principal landmark. As communications improved, with the building of a road and then a railway, which by 1870 extended to Warsaw, and finally the arrival of the Bornholm and Karlskrona steamboats, the German, Polish and Scandinavian aristocracy and wealthy bourgeoisie decided that this was the perfect place for a summer home. Blessed with beaches of fine sand and green hills, in the 1920s the resort once again enjoyed phenomenal success, benefiting now from the opening of a casino and the Grand Hotel.

Sopot began another chapter in its history in 1998, when it was refurbished as a spa and seaside resort within an independent Poland. For Eva and Michal Herman, this revival was the opportunity to realize a long-held dream of opening an art gallery where they would exhibit their own and their friends' work, their clientele drawn from passers-by in the town's quiet streets.

Eager to get started and make contacts, the two artists found the ideal location on Heroes of Monte Cassino Street, Sopot's main artery, and moved in. They soon realized that sitting there waiting for passing trade was just not their style. To attract visitors and provoke some sort of reaction, they turned the gallery into a restaurant, which they called the Blue Poodle (*Blekitny Pudel*) – the eccentric decor of which aroused comment from the start.

On the walls, mock family photos coexist with paintings ancient and modern, while the furnishings are more typical of a bohemian apartment than a restaurant. At the Blue Poodle, every object seems to celebrate the glories of Sopot in its heyday, no doubt appropriate now that the town's fortunes are again on the up and up....

PAGES 130–131: Even at the entrance, the visitor is confronted with an eclectic and incongruous mix of objects. The street cobbles have crept inside the house, and solid doors are replaced with metal gates.

ABOVE AND OPPOSITE: Russian wallpaper of a faded splendour, armchairs upholstered with worn leather, oil lamps, sewing machine, telephone and transistor radio dating from the days of recession – these make up the old-fashioned decor of the salon. These oddly familiar objects evoke a powerful sense of nostalgia.

OPPOSITE AND ABOVE: Amidst this
surreal assembly of bric-a-brac is
a collection of shoe lasts (above),
a bust of Karl Marx, a birdcage
and the cornice of an armoire, set
above a doorway. Portrait photos
and a few paintings by artist friends
fit perfectly into a decorative
scheme that has a curiously
haunting beauty (opposite).

Lithuania

OPPOSITE: Grasses, twigs, leaves and seeds collected on the beaches or in the forest, washed by the waves and dried in the wind, are the elements from which Kristina Danilevicius creates her compositions. Set against a paper background washed with cool or sandy colour, the graphic interplay of the plant materials, simply glued on to the surface, evokes the landscape of the dunes and the grasses blowing in the wind.

ABOVE: On returning from her solitary and contemplative quests out in the bracing sea air, Kristina likes nothing more than to sit in front of the crackling fire, surrounded by objects from the natural world.

Latvia

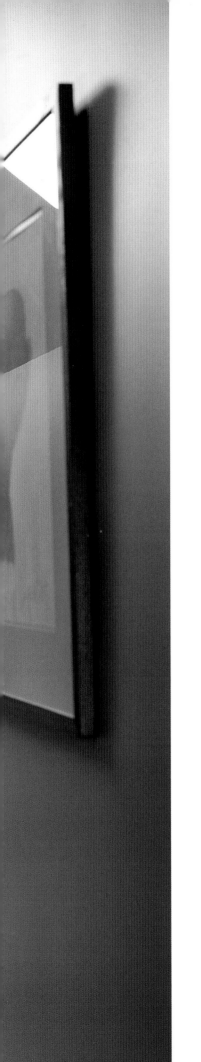

OPPOSITE: There is a definite flavour
of the cabin deck about this upstairs
corridor with its openwork doors
and yacht varnish on the oak floors –
a conscious or unconscious reference
to all the summers Zaiga and Maris
have spent on their boat.
RIGHT: The painting by Boris
Berzins is a good example of the
non-academic style of Latvian art.
It shares the space with a traditional
icon (above).

Estonian manor houses are set deep within the forest, potent reminders of the days when the scions of the Baltic German aristocracy established in the region used to go hunting for brown bears, wild boar and lynxes. From 1238 to 1346, Estonia had been under Danish rule, before it was ceded to the Swordbrothers. Two hundred German merchants from Gotland were invited in to settle on the shores of the Gulf of Finland, their task to transform Tallinn ('town of the Danes') into a springboard for Hanseatic trade with Russia. Neither Swedish dominion in the 16th century nor rule by tsarist Russia from the 18th century caused more than a ripple in the estates held by the Baltic Germans, which continued to function as the granary for Western Europe.

Alas, few of the manor houses dating from Sweden's golden age escaped destruction in the Great War of the North in the early 18th century. A frenzy of reconstruction took place in the 18th and 19th centuries which tended to favour the neoclassical, neo-Renaissance, neo-Gothic and ultimately, in the early 20th century, Jugendstil or Art Nouveau.

While the rulers of the Baltic countries pursued their territorial squabbles, the Estonian peasants clung on both to their land and their Finno-Ugric language. Out in the countryside Estonian culture flourished, serving as a spearhead for national revival in the 19th century. The same ancestral tradition that resisted Nazi and Soviet oppression in the 20th century is today the guarantee of Estonia's independent identity within a wider Europe: this young nation is proud of its architectural heritage and eager to restore it to its former splendour.

PAGES 156–157: A view of Haapsalu Bay.

OPPOSITE: A villa in the resort of Haapsalu, once the favourite summer destination of the tsars, has now been turned into a restaurant.
RIGHT: A detail of a bow window in Tallinn's main street.
FAR RIGHT: Houses in Haapsalu.

With its long beaches
of fine white sand,
Pärnu Bay is popular
for seaside holidays,
but an artist couple
have chosen an
old farmhouse as
their summer home.

Like many dream homes, Sepamaa apparently chose its owners rather than the other way around, first luring them to the spot, then placing a few minor obstacles in their way to test the strength of their conviction, before surrendering itself unreservedly. And it did not choose just anyone: it chose an artist couple, Jaak Arro, a native of the region, and Epp Maria Kokamägi, who at once felt this was where she belonged. The old farmhouse, once the home of the village blacksmith (Sepamaa means 'home of the blacksmith'), was little more than a dilapidated ruin when the couple began bit by bit to domesticate it, back in those Soviet days when everything was in short supply.

Epp Maria is well known for her paintings of angels and has a passion for sky blue. Tongues began to wag in the village when she started to paint everything from the walls and doors to the floors and even the furniture in the very colour that was identified in people's minds with their former Russian occupiers. The Russians believed that if the door was blue, God would enter, and so they adopted the old Orthodox practice and used it as the colour for the doors and shutters of their homes. But Epp Maria stuck to her guns. At the time, it was far from easy to get hold of the materials needed to renovate the house: in the middle of a recession, it was a major endeavour to source the rolls of ancient gilded wallpaper that now cover the upper part of the walls.

For these two artists, one of the great things about the farmhouse was its stable, which they converted into a summer studio. As the light does not reach this magnificent space until the afternoon, the days tend to start gently with a bathe in the sea and a walk along the beach by the juniper trees, followed by breakfast cooked on the stove in the old-fashioned way. Maybe a few minutes in the garden tending the tomatoes and basil plants, then Epp Maria paints in the studio while Jaak sculpts in the garden. In the summer, the days are long and the light lasts forever. Friends come to share the unique atmosphere and sit around the samovar with them late into the night in the lamplight under the apple trees.

But their favourite time in Pärnu is Midsummer's Day. Epp Maria and her daughters put on traditional full red skirts for the occasion. Seven white flowers representing the birth of summer are slid under the girls' pillows, so they will see their future sweetheart in their dreams. It is the summer solstice, the longest day, and everyone is impatient for the night when big wood fires will be lit on the beach to frighten away evil spirits. Tradition has it that you burn an old boat, planting it upright in the sand so the flames leap high in the sky. Another favourite activity is catching fireflies, which Epp Maria compares to falling stars. Autumn always seems to come too soon, making them retreat indoors, where they have their own work and paintings by Epp Maria's parents for company.

ABOVE (TOP): Estonian farmhouses traditionally comprised a single long building on one level where animals and people lived adjacent to one another. The outer door led straight into the kitchen, which marked the division between living quarters and stable.

ABOVE (BOTTOM): A bas-relief by Jaak Arro leans against the stable wall. The comfortable proportions of these traditional farmhouses make them very much sought after today as second homes.

OPPOSITE: In summer, a wooden table and benches are set out under the branches of the big apple tree, creating an improvised dining room in the garden. If possible they like to eat all their meals in their 'outdoors room', often joined by the many friends who pass through – artists, writers and actors who appreciate the Chekhovian atmosphere.

ABOVE: Home to a painter, the old farmhouse displays the full gamut of colours. In the bedroom, panelling, floor and chairs are all painted sky blue, Epp Maria's favourite colour.
RIGHT: The sitting room benefits from warmer tones, browns and reds with ultramarine accents.
OPPOSITE: Until the autumn, the house is heated by two stoves: one modern, in heat-resistant stone, which Epp Maria uses for cooking; the other, with wrought-iron doors, used purely for warmth.

ABOVE AND OPPOSITE: In Estonia, it was the custom for women to wear different costumes according to their village of origin. With a strict code of dress distinguishing girls, married women and widows, there was a huge variety of styles. Even today the womenfolk of a small island off Pärnu wear their costume all the time, for fishing or for working in the fields.

On Midsummer's Day, Epp Maria and her daughters like to don their full striped skirts (above) for the traditional celebration of the summer solstice. The superb portrait of a peasant woman (above) is the work of Epp Maria's father, Luulik Kokamägi, while the large painting on the wall (opposite) was done by Epp Maria herself.

OPPOSITE AND RIGHT: 'The artists have taken over the cowshed!' exclaims Epp Maria with a laugh, referring to the summer studio in the converted stable (right). Once the doors are opened wide to let in the light, there is no real demarcation between inside and out, just a marvellous sense of freedom. This is where Epp Maria paints the angels for which she is famous, and Jaak sculpts his bas-reliefs, although he often prefers to work in the garden rather than clutter up the studio. Upstairs, a bedroom is installed in the well-lit, tranquil space that has been created underneath the handsome timber-frame roof (opposite and top right).

OVERLEAF: Sepamaa's private beach on Pärnu Bay.

OPPOSITE AND ABOVE: The original of the ladder was spotted in an interior decoration magazine. The sisters had six of them made for hanging up towels and linen. The side table with branches for legs has been so successful that it is now being sold in a limited edition.

The sauna was based on a quick sketch by Ristomatti Ratia. The interior architect had been invited to dinner and simply drew it on a corner of the table while Piri was putting the finishing touches to the food.

You ladle water from the wooden bucket on to the hot stones until the temperature reaches 80˚C, then beat yourself gently with a bundle of twigs previously immersed in water. Here oak twigs are used as a substitute for the more traditional birch.

Finland

PAGES 186–187: An area of the aquarium, the annexe to the children's house.

OPPOSITE AND ABOVE: Long and low, the main house is inspired by the style of Lapp architecture. A terrace runs along the south-facing façade (above). The foundations were dug by local fishermen, and the chalet was then assembled more or less like a Lego kit. All the materials were brought in by boat, and the men lived under canvas while the work was done. There is another small terrace on the east side (opposite) that is sheltered from the wind, ensuring a sea view in all weathers.

OPPOSITE: Wood is the dominant material, inside and out, with few textiles to be seen. A softer note is introduced by sheepskins thrown over Kaare Klint's Safari chairs that grace the sitting-room.

ABOVE: One of the fundamental architectural principles in this part of the world is to use your energy sources economically. Solar power suffices for lighting, but only just; for heating, the main house relies on the fire in the hearth, which interconnects with the stove in the kitchen and a small wooden sauna.

RIGHT: On the terrace stand the big wooden casks once used as brine tubs by the fishermen, who used to pickle Baltic herring and sea birds for their own consumption.

ABOVE AND RIGHT: The objects left
behind by the previous occupants
make up a little museum collection
of their own, including fishing nets,
slippers of woven birch bark (above)
and a wooden cask of the type used
by sailors to store their clothes in the
dry (right).

OPPOSITE: The granite stone walls of
the old stable were incorporated into
the children's house, known as the
church. The simple yet effective
table and chairs were made by Heikki.
As in the main house, traditional rag
runners decorate the floors. The
stepladder up to the children's
sleeping area was hewn out of
a single tree trunk.

OPPOSITE (TOP): The smoke sauna has its origins in Finland's ancient shamanistic forests. Imported to the archipelago, it incorporates modifications to compensate for the shortage of wood. The roof hidden under its covering of grass is very nearly flat and the layer of plant material much thicker than would have been used on one of the old granaries. And there is no question here of separate compartments for smoking meat or fish, just a single space to which you can retire and enjoy a gentle perfumed warmth before plunging into the nearby sea. In summer the ceremony is performed daily, no doubt much to the delight of visitors who have dropped anchor for the night.

OPPOSITE (BOTTOM LEFT): The perforated planks of a fish tank, used by the fishermen who previously inhabited the island to transport live fish back to the shore.

ABOVE: The landing stage.

RIGHT: The spartan comforts of the outside toilet.

OVERLEAF: Facing south-west, the sheltered terrace has a view of the setting sun.

OPPOSITE: When Magnus Linder II moved to Svartå with his young wife in 1783, only the ground floor was habitable. The Gustavian furniture, although subsequently added to, dates largely from the period of their occupation.

ABOVE: The elegant table in the dining room recalls the grand dinners of the period, at which distinguished visitors would be served Madeira and fine wines.

RIGHT: However much they might have liked costly parquet and silk curtains, the norm was making do with linen and pine planks with a squared design in imitation of a parquet floor.

ABOVE AND OPPOSITE: The Linder family are the owners of a major art collection, evidence both of their social rank and excellent taste. Baron Fridolf Linder was an enthusiastic archaeologist who in the second half of the 19th century collected more than three hundred Stone Age objects, which he left to the museum in Turku.

Hjalmar Linder covered the walls of the manor house with some distinguished works of art, including paintings by Rembrandt and Joshua Reynolds. He was a generous patron to Finnish painters of the late 19th century, purchasing Albert Edelfelt's *White Queen* and commissioning work from his brother-in-law, Louis Sparre. In the 1920s, he presented his valuable collections to the Finnish Museum of Fine Arts.

A garden city on the
Helsinki archipelago,
Kulosaari offers all
the pleasures of living
by the sea in the heart
of the capital.

It is a legendary house created by a legendary couple, Antti and Vuokko Nurmesniemi, two figures at the forefront of Nordic style in the 1960s and 1970s – one as an architect, the other as a designer, working in fashion, glass and ceramics. The house was built when they were at the peak of their success, and it remains quite unchanged; even the paintings are original. Yet it is not that the house has become marooned in the past, rather that it has become a design classic, a style archetype. The huge bright space, with large glazed bays, and the waxed blond wood of Finnish forests interact with its environment. So perfectly thought through and executed that nothing has been modified over the years and nothing added except a library.

Antti Nurmesniemi was taking a huge gamble. A house that was 500 metres square: a single space with no internal dividing walls, except for the bedroom, and put together like an industrial building, with twelve pillars and a steel frame. When the first snow arrived and lasted several weeks, Antti got worried and called the foreman: 'Call back if it's still snowing in six months,' came the reply. In the event, the flat roof (a bold stroke in the northern Baltic) has never once leaked. In those years of oil shortages, Antti was also worried about the loss of heat in such a large space. Triple glazing was installed and underfloor heating as well as radiators, but it has never been used. And similarly the air conditioning, introduced in case the building overheated like a greenhouse, has also proved superfluous.

So, a single volume, with virtually no doors or partitions. The living spaces – entrance hall, dining room, kitchen, sauna and living room – are subtly demarcated by differences of level. Everything is calculated to the nearest millimetre, including the furniture. Few objects, and those that do exist are hidden away in cupboards that are rarely opened. Not many pictures, and not because there are few walls to hang them on, but because they would seem almost incongruous in this open space.

With its unencumbered outlook, nature and the sea are much in evidence. After ten summers, Antti and Vuokko parted with their old holiday home, certain that Kulosaari (Brandö) was the place for them. Perhaps because together they had created the modern equivalent of something architects had dreamed of as far back as the late 19th century: a garden city, where the Swiss chalet look was abandoned in favour of houses built of the Art Nouveau materials of brick and stone, so that they could be lived in all year round.

For Vuokko, as she talks about her island, the house is filled with memories of her husband Antti. With its parks where you can ski in winter and a casino with one of the finest views of Helsinki, Kulosaari is an exceptional place to live, just a few minutes from the town centre. 'Do you know,' she adds, 'that in winter the connections are even quicker, because the buses go from island to island over the frozen sea? Finland is the only country in the world where you can do that.'

PAGE 215: Originally designed in 1952 by Antti Nurmesniemi for Helsinki's Palace Hotel, the stools in the sauna have become huge bestsellers. Inspired by the three-legged stools traditionally used for milking, their combination of extreme formal simplicity with natural wood has made them modern icons.

RIGHT: Most of the seating was designed by Antti.

OPPOSITE: On the floor above, a space for relaxation. One of the walls has been replaced by a series of glazed bays, an architectural solution that encourages the sense of being at one with nature.

Pages 218–219: The dining room has the same minimalist decor as the rest of the house. It occupies the intermediate level and adjoins the kitchen.

Above: With its starkly geometric lines, the pine staircase inhabits its space like a sculpture. Reduced to its simplest expression, the ramp turns into a shelf at the base. On the bench, a hat, a souvenir of Vuokko's early days when she was a designer for Marimekko. In the boutique that bears her name on the Esplanade in Helsinki, Vuokko still displays her brightly coloured fashions.

Opposite: After a sauna and a few reviving lengths in the swimming pool, relaxation is the theme in the adjacent seating area, which is situated below sea level.

Sølvi dos Santos would like to express her deepest thanks to all those people, often complete strangers, who opened the doors of their homes to her and helped her in every way possible. This book is dedicated to them as an expression of her sincere gratitude.

Translated from the French, *Maisons de la Baltique*, by Jane Brenton

First published in the United Kingdom in 2005 by Thames & Hudson Ltd, 181A High Holborn, London WC1V 7QX

www.thamesandhudson.com

Original version © 2004 Éditions du Chêne, France
This edition © 2005 Thames & Hudson Ltd, London

British Library Cataloguing-in-Publication Data
A catalogue record for this book is available from the British Library

ISBN-13: 978-0-500-51220-3

ISBN-10: 0-500-51220-5

Printed and bound in Hong Kong